The Strippers pocketbook

Putting a breath of fresh air into your relationship

Contents

2017 © Lars Mundi
Publisher: BoD – Copenhagen, Denmark
Printing: BoD – Norderstedt, Germany
ISBN: 978-87-7188-402-9

Disclaimer

This statement is for everyone who purchases or reviews this book. The author and publishers of this book will not be held responsible for any acts committed in lieu of this book. These acts were performed by a professional and you should not try these shows with unqualified professionals. Should you proceed to try this at home, we, the author and publishers will not be held accountable. The author and publishers of this book would like you to know that they will not be held responsible for you or your actions should you act or otherwise try anything suggested within this book.

There is a degree of nudity in the pictures within this book. These were pictures taken of a certified professional. The author and publishers do not condone your actions if you try something like this at home. We will not be held accountable to what you may think is cause for your inferior decisions from the reading of this book. Thank you.

Introduction!

This booklet is intended, as a breath of fresh air for those who think your relationship needs a little something extra.

Maybe one of your friends wants to have a few fun experiences. Again remember, if it is a friend, to be sure he or she knows their limits. You should respect theirs just as well as they should respect your boundaries. However, having said that, feel good with it. Remember, everyone loves surprises in life whether it is men or women.

We may enjoy that others have thought of us and put us in the limelight. It is the same way with stripping. Putting the person that you have selected for the job to get the experience. He or she would love this to be done for them and that you are someone who gives them this experience will make all the difference.

My desire with this book is not to teach you to go out into the world to become stripper and have it as a profession. However, I would like to give you an opportunity, to give a little extra into your relationship and, allow you to be the star for a night with the magic that comes with good feelings.

I myself have been a stripper and made myself in this world for 6 years by a number of different companies both here at home and also in Sweden. I have many experiences from that time. I sometimes get to thinking about these experiences and smile to myself.

I will later in the book tell a little of that time and share some of the experiences you can have. I hope you can get some enjoyment out of reading this and could use it for spicing up your life. I hope that you can give some joy to the partner you have. I hope you take this as fresh input, and it may well be you find out something you do not know or would like to try. I hope that you will like what you see and have a good reading.

Lars Rex Mundi

Preface!

I welcome you to my book and although I am heterosexual, my desire with this book is to stimulate all sexes no matter what sexuality you may have. That you can and will make use of a few techniques, that are in this book to give pleasure to those as you choose to be part of your shows if only your partner. There is this magic moment that will give everybody this special moment and no one should judge you for that. I have chosen to shed some light on these areas that are part of the erotic universe that we all are part of in some way.

If you have a different sexuality than heterosexual, this book is going to fill you with inspiration and joy in your life. I can only rejoice at this. For me, it is not about what sexual orientation you are when you read this book. I hope you get out what was intended for you. For me there is no right or wrong sexuality between adults. As long as you are having fun and able to give yourself to your partner. Yes, I have achieved what I wanted with the book. Therefore, it is just for you, that I write the book for this reason.

Lars Rex Mundi

Chapter 1: The erotic universe!

The erotic universe is interesting and diverse in many ways. All people encounter this at some point in their adult life. It helps to enrich us as human beings whether we are men or whether we are women. The erotic universe also has some taboos associated with this which helps to create any myths that may have no basis in reality. Someone once said, "we keep ourselves as human beings just to find out whether there is anything in our prejudices."

I found some prejudices when I worked as a stripper. Although we in Denmark (who are very liberal) feel very sexual. There are still some prejudices that still cling to people and their point of view. There may be many reasons why people do it that way, and maybe they do not do away with prejudices about other people.

I am an ordinary person who has taken a slightly different choice. For it was a completely different world to work in as a stripper. As I mentioned I was an ordinary person. I was a bit shy with the opposite sex, as so many other people are. I love to be social with my friends and share different experiences that are associated with having friends. Whatever it meant to hang out with my friends was many different things. I enjoy going out to eat, going to the movies and, going into the city. Yes, I play also role-play what are called pen and paper. It is a great way to be with others and solve problems that may arise in the game. Actually, I was an ordinary person who differed only by my little different industry as a stripper.

As I mentioned, the erotic universe has changed a great deal. Whatever one's sexuality might be and what you want in this universe. For there are many opportunities for you to explore and enrich yourselves and the person or persons you choose to be part of these experiences. There are many different forms of sexuality; the best known is heterosexual, as most people know. However, there are also bisexual, gay, transgender, pan sexual, or one of many other directions as may be in this universe. Then the experiences you grow enrich you as the person you are, as long as one chooses to have respect for both yourself and your partner.

A small part of the erotic universe and aspects of the erotic is actually, what I have written this book as a stripper. I hope you have done away with your own prejudices you might have about being a stripper. I will be happy if you choose to take some of the things I mention in your own way to create a little joy in your life both for yourself and for others who are in your life.

Denmark was one of the first countries in the world that released porn but also released the abortion. It is not that the two things go hand in hand with each other. This gave some debate between different groups and some of these groups perceived these things wrong and immoral in relation to the perception they have on this matter. It is really that many Danes have a relaxed attitude to nudity and is very open about talking about sexuality, and in many ways, it is one of the things, I do enjoy about living in a country like Denmark. Where it often seems that we must embark on what is perceived as taboo inside of the erotic universe between adult humans.

Although there is some sexuality I do understand, that there is a more natural relationship to it than that which hides it away. People do not want to talk about it or come into contact with it because they see it as something negative or banned. Although this openness on the field is not equal, we mean to be involved in these things. Nevertheless, that one is free to approach and talk about what are the motives of other people who perceive these things in a different way.

Chapter 2: How to get started!

It is always a big jump from talking about the idea to become a stripper and then to be in the limelight. How do you get involved? For there is not an easy way to do this. I will just try to see if I can make it possible for you to when to you take the plunge into it. Yes, it is easier to say than to do. However, that is how it is as with everything in life and very often we would like as a person, to have it all given without having to work for it. Yes, where it would be nice in every way if it were given that option. Again, reality is at any time a little hard and therefore easy to give up, for so many of us is that we are up and running with it, as it was the desire to start with.

The biggest obstacle that victims have with us as human beings is our inner voice. It always tells us something that is negative or otherwise to us that the person we have to give up what we have in mind. It may be a thought that we are too thick or not trained enough or do not have the correct form to get started stripping. However, it is not only at this point that the inner voice, makes us give up on the desire that we do have here in life. It could be to invite someone out when the fear comes in over and over. The inner voice interrupts our thoughts and gets us to abandon our desire.

I will try to give you some tips and some techniques that may help you to get on and get started, within this area and in other areas in life you can use them. For you are not only specific to this area. It is not only intended for this and you can use it for other areas of your life. So yes, I am just glad there is nothing better than people who are successful in life and it gives me an inner joy to hear or to experience this to some degree for some people to get success.

As Sun Tzu mentions in his book, 'the art of war'. "So is the worst enemy of your enemy that can break you at any time." I often find I am holding it all back to go out and do things. How often have I heard that if it were not because this, I would do or another form of apology that would keep you back to grip an experience or an opportunity to succeed in your life.

Yes, I think you deserve to get the best in life. However, remember, I cannot do it for you. You even have to go a step in that direction and take the challenge that may come along the way. It is also about looking at the challenges that may be in your life in relation to the assignment or desire you have in terms of reaching your goals. For indeed it is always more pleasant to be in the finish than to be out there fighting the battle. If everything was so easy, we would all be successful in life. However, it just is not and you are often forced to fight any battles and choose the right techniques to the finishing line as a winner of its desire.

I will try to give you one of the many techniques that are out on the market, for there is a part and which I mention here is one of them I have used and which I find pretty easy and quick to make use of. For very often, it is the brain that comes into play and inputs many thoughts, and often but not always, to control some of the things that come into play in our lives and this has an ability to receive a negative outcome which in no way is positive. Not to say that it always going to happen but so many times we play in our brains in a negative way and it affects us as the people we are.

For remember that the brain is an amazing thing. One has the ability to make his or her own perception to make us give up the things they want or you may have in your life. You might think it would be nice to have in your life. I have also want to talk about the techniques that can be used, and which I have used one of them that is out there. When your brain starts making horror scenarios and causes one to pause, it is important that you stop and take the dialogue with the brain. For it has an ability to control one's progress in life. If this is the situation that is unpleasant for us and unfamiliar for our system.

Here can I get in on a technique that I have used some different places in my life. When the brain starts to play with its fear as in all manners, it very often makes us abandon the front yard we need. Then I think I had better get with it when the brain makes its foray into the situations you are in. You must take a dialogue with the inner voice and determine if it is not the worst, that you will get it. Whatever it may be and in the beginning, it is always difficult but after trying it a few times to take its effect. Suddenly you begin to relax your body and you become clearer because your brain accepts what you are facing. Well, what is the worst that could happen for example if you were to strip? That your partner might not think that you live up to his or her expectations, but are you now sure that he or she does not just do you think is the nicest because you give him or her this experience? Remember sometimes there must be very small things to create this change.

Chapter 3: I need a fantasy!

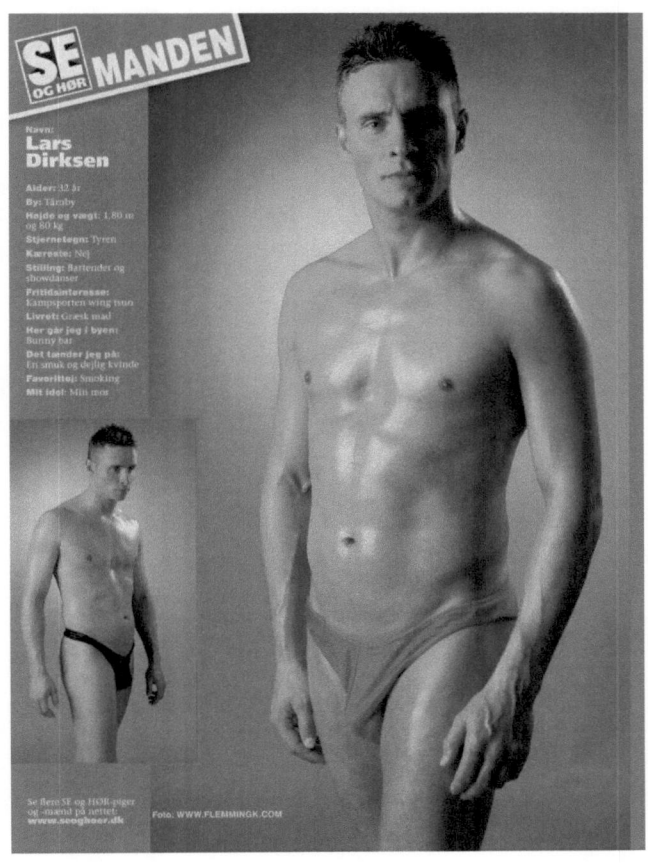

Imagination has always come into play with us people going through life. It is not only when it comes to a strip show but actually in all areas of life. Who cannot remember one's youth love if you have not had many fantasies. As you fulfill one's joys to experience the person who sharing your life is really special and unique.

It is in the same way with a strip show. You have to find out which fantasy your partner has in this area, and what desires they have. For we all have fantasies that can make us feel alive and we would like to experience.

It would be better if this were a fantasy, which one had suddenly become a reality and that was an experience. For some of the fantasies that you have outlived, you can still remember many years after and they can still bring joy in our minds. So, one should not hold back to being shared.

Remember to smile and use it as a magic weapon, when you make your show and yes, it is hard to smile. However, here I will give you a little advice to help me when I myself was stripper. When one smiles and is happy, it also expressed through your eyes and yes, it is hard to change one's attitude. If the most of life has been a perception of oneself as less than attractive, charmless and awkward. I will give you this advice and yes it works and has a big effect on how you must strip, or just being among other normal people.

It is always hard to get to smile as a person; especially if it is not something, you have done very much in life. The smile should most often come from within. So now, you got one of my secrets that I have used for many years and with great success. You have to find something that can get you to be happy and yes here, a mischievous imagination can be worth gold. I do not know what your fantasies are but I know you must use your imagination here. Whatever it may be, and with this idea you should use it when you meet other people. You must also use it on your strip show as the secret weapon that could always have made a big difference.

It is always difficult to have to start something new, but it can succeed if you act on it. If you work with it, it should probably come far and yes, it is going to take some time and some of your energy. However, it is of equal worth spending some time in this direction, and remember it may well, be you getting ones' experiences afterwards that you should not forget. Again, remember that it also should be fun to just do it.
When you are at work in this area, look for which imagination your partner has. There are many places you could look for this and find what you need. Just to mention some, if you could you look at the film as he or she chooses to see, for there is almost, always a heartthrob who has something specific. Clothes, body parts, or you could look at any of the many exotic magazines that are intended explicitly for men or women.

There are usually some pictures in these magazines, but you can of course also choose to ask what they would hold dear about the fantasies. Therefore, you have a little to work with. Also, so you know in which direction your show must go, and what you should spend your time on and where you need to be your most energetic. There are many ways to get his or her partner to reveal their fantasies, because we all have some sort of fantasies that you would like to have lived out.

Yes, there may be several reasons why they have not been done, been said or, told of their imagination. In addition, what is the reason for this? Yes, it is a good question. There may be several reasons for what has not has been done, been said, or told of their imagination. And what the reason is for this so it is a good question. If you choose to be open about this then set to find out what this fantasy is.

If you have not figured out what their fantasy is, I will here give some different proposals. As I have experienced those women, have that on the one side, somehow found a naughty fantasy, and brought them to life and made this person really turned on by it. There is, the police officer, the firefighter but also the military officer, preferably in white; it will have a magical effect on some women or men. Who is the goal of this fantasy and imagination? Is it come to life for the person, you are stripping for? Therefore, if you have not been lucky at this point then you could do a little more research, or, start here and then move on out of the line. Still remember your magic weapon is the winning smile.

     I would recommend that you read a bit about the group you have selected, more so you know a little more about what type they are. Yes, it is not necessary but equally well, it could be a little fun, that you have done a little work in this field. What do they have as tools in their work, if it is a firefighter? He has such. An ax and also boots just to mention some of the things that might imply to be a firefighter.

After you find out which fantasy you intend to do, it may not matter what it is. Let us take the output, that it is, a firefighter you choose. Which should be your show for your partner. Therefore, it is important that you find everything there is about a firefighter, and yes, you may use the myth of this profession in your strip show. Moreover, find out what props that might be used, plus to use such things as oil, and other things you use in your show. There are many choices at this point, and yes, it is your imagination, that sets the limits.

Remember another thing which is important. I will just mention it here before I forget it. Remember, when you have made your show, you can also use it elsewhere in life. You must always think of something you find sexy. It could be a fantasy, you once lived out, or someone you think something sexy about who is waiting for you somewhere. When you do this, think of this fantasy about this person, you that are going to make you smile, and get the twinkle in your eye. As if there are right moments in time to use this ability to be turned on. This is the magic moment, which we can act as a success for those who use it.

A poster from the old days, from my Indiana Jones strip show

Chapter 4: Props and things, that can be used, in a strip show!

There are many things, you can use in a strip show. Yes, it is only your imagination, that sets limits to what one cannot use, and in what way they should be used, against the one the stripper is facing. However, I will go through some of the more normal props, that you can start using.

When you choose to use props, and how one can use them, and in which context. If you have some idea, then just use them and remember, it is your show so you decide what is to be in it for content. How it should look and in which direction you want it to move to accent your style.

In fact, as I mentioned you will use everything in a strip show. Nevertheless, right in the beginning, it may be difficult. However, it comes with time and practice like the rehearsal you will do in this area. However, by that practice, I mean not just once. You can be better at this point. It will be easier to find different things, (if you practice) and not just what you had intended to spend in this direction could be used. Because you come to think differently than before, it is clear that when you enter a new area of his or her life. It could be a job, which you have not tried before, or into a new relationship. Then you will always be a little insecure in the new relationships that is going to happen in one's life.

However, in this chapter, I will examine what could be used for various props. You could choose to strip with props. How they could be used, and yes with a little imagination on your part should probably get to have the power, which will give joy to your partner and will sure reward you later. For this is all you need to please each other in a relationship, and this is only one among many ways to please his or her partner. However, I had better return to the props used. And later, I could touch on other things you also might use and get some fun out of it. More so, you are going to be able to communicate as a stripper.

For all equipment, can be used in strip show. Although some things are, better in this area than others, as you will find out. It also comes along on what type of show to build, and which items should be in it. In addition, what should be contained in your strip show. If it should be a fun strip show, one can use music that nobody really takes seriously stripping to. This could well be a local folk singer and yes, I have even stripped to this type of music, even if it became a very strange strip show. In addition, got someone to smile about it. That is another story, I might tell later in the book.

What kind of music do I use for a show?

There are many types of music to use, when doing a strip show. There are many types of music and some of them can be used with great success. The real effect to have in mind is to create just the right mood. For one of the things that often create the effect is music. You can just look at the film and the way music plays in it, or look at how the people of a city react to it. It has an effect on us, and it is this effect you need when you are going to make a strip number, to others or the person you have in mind

You can always find out what the other person likes. In addition, if there is any number, which has some of the memories, so use them and create the real effect. When you are completing your show, you could play some soft music, such as a song as Marc Anthony: "You sang to me". Alternatively, this other song of him: "When I dream at night". If you choose a sensitive end of your strip show. Remember that music is only a proposal and it is again up to you, to find some music that you just seem fit for the show you choose to implement.

When you put your strip show together with the music. Always play a big role, and here I will just give more advice. When the stripper will normally be working it, it is between 10 to 15 minutes long. It is hard to run it much farther than this. Because if it is running longer than that, it very often becomes a dull experience. The people or the person who looks at who comes next is always bored, the entire center act is failing and it loses its magic. It is not what you want. It is better to make it short and still keep the magic alive.

Find some music that the person you choose to strip to likes also that you like. Again, it is best if there are some memories associated with the music; it gives it a little extra magic to your strip show. However, I will leave it up to you, to choose what you find works for you. It is you, who must strip not me. The time is over for me but I thought it was a fun time. Remember that it will be good to have a three-track minimum, on a CD or other things, which you have to play your music from.

Oil!

One of the things I used was oil, and the oil is the same you used when you a getting a massage. Therefore, that leads thoughts towards something, which has pleased to do. There is something magical about the liquid, above the water, and above other things, which could lead our imagination in a sly direction. When you use oil on your body, it is important, for you get close to his or her lap and he or she is allowed to feel you and your body. Let him or her reach to your body all the while looking deep into his or her eyes, this moment could also be magic. You can control his or her hands where it should enhance the mood.

Remember that the eyes are the way to the soul, and very often, the eyes of others fascinate us. When we look at a person and how one can use the eyes in many ways. Others used their eyes at you in the same way, any time it was conscious and other times it was not. However, when stripping you may use your eyes, to play with and seduce the person you are stripping for, and lead him or her to where they are lost in the show you made.

There are many types of oil out on the market, which you can use and get the best out of a show. How you choose to buy your oil is up to you to find out. However, I have often bought my oil in the local stores, where you can get these goods and they can be sure to find one that is right for your tastes and needs.

People who sell scented oil may have suggestions as to what may be a good smell to produce a certain mood but you decide what may be best for you.

Candle!

There are many types of candles, which can be used for this purpose. I myself prefer to use the thick candle, but again it is a personal matter. What it is used for most and yes, it is all about trial and error in this area. What the purpose of using candles is, is to pour it on yourself, and allow to it have an effect. We could mention another place but it is for the same purpose, as it is with other types of liquid. Candles are often associated with something pleasant, or romanticism.   So, remember that this could also have an effect on it as watching the show, and when to use it, I had chosen to describe in another chapter. Again, scented candles might enhance the mood. What is his or her favorite smell?

Use water!

In my time as a stripper, I found that water, was a good thing to have in my show. It could be used in many ways to highlight some different things. Think about your own body, when I mention this. Therefore, I will try to describe it here as best I can. Water has always been fascinating for us as humans. Just to mention that someone gets things as, for example, Madonna: "Cherish" video, wherein the water plays an important role and has nothing magic about it, and you can sure find other music video which use water as the main themes.

It is the imagination with that when the second pair is wet, then their clothes too wet and it is natural to happen is that one's clothes, going to reveal something that I am playing with a fantasy. Both men and women have the ability to find it also in use in the film Spiderman, where there is a scene in the film where Kirsten Dunst is in the rain weather, and when it rains heavily and reveals how her beautiful body looks. However, again without actually knows for sure again that is being played on the imagination and this is one of the important things to play on the imagination. Then use the water to create a bold imagination before you exit your show.

You can have a bowl that you can pour over yourself, so your clothes are going to reveal something that cannot possibly be seen. It is also possible to use a water bottle that you use in a gym; shoots water into the air and let it hit your upper body, finished before you have thrown your shirt. If you make it, last you can always use the water on your body, same with your hands on your body. Use it so they get to see your sensitive side, and so it seems that you really like what you do by yourself. It does not matter you are play-acting that this is a treat for you, and yes it has its effect as they're looking at and seeing it.

What type of clothes for my show!

When you choose clothes for your show, there is a great selection to go for when you will strip. There are many different varieties of costumes to choose among. It can be uniforms of any kind, such as firefighter, police officer, gentleman or other after your fantasy. It is only imagination, that puts a stop to it, and even if it is not possible to acquire just as easily the type of costume, you can always find a needle, and thread back and then create it that way. It also means that you can make it the way you want it.

You must equally well find it forward, when you need to make your pants with Velcro to be part of the side of your pants. When you pull them apart during your show. But you will have ample opportunity to find out how it works, when you need to practice. Yes, you will take too long to put your pants together again. and yes, uniforms are a little price heavy but can be overpriced when you have to work within this field.

Again, if you have an idea for a show, but do not know where you can get your equipment along you can always jump on the internet, and find out how you can order it. Otherwise, there is always the option to go to your local shop. They have a huge variety of different things and with just a little imagination, could turn into a uniform. You just stand to and create exactly what those strip shows need that you have in mind. That will give joy that night to whoever gets to see it.

Shoes!

Shoes can also be used in an erotic way, and yes, it is very simple and yes, I know it is probably not exactly what you think when you look at shoes. That it also has an option to create something different, and yes, I will describe your card here and although it might sound strange, then the person who experiences it remembers it very clearly.

I will tell the story where I used shoes as an object so that it become a part of my strip show. I know so many people here also among people who are interested in politics. It is not my point to have any political message with what I write, but some of you will become part of it and tell a story. However, I was contacting an acquaintance of mine (from LAU) is from a youth political party, who knew that I worked as a stripper at that time and asked me. I could not help them to make a period of Radikal Venstre, which is another political party, and the optional video where a male stripper for Zenia Stampe, which is one of the people selected in Danish politics.

When I came to my shoes, I used them in an erotic way, and the young lady that was filming this strip show for the video said afterward, "I will never be able to look at a pair of shoes the same way". I have used my shoes on and in an erotic direction. I have the jerk shoes and so is the debt for when using your belt use it the same way eroticism. Instead of just let it fall off so create a little tension around it, and yes you can use it in many ways and again it is up to you, I'm just trying to come up with a little input on your account here.

I was a stripper in a youth political party in one of their videos on demand, which ended up getting in the press, and yes, people do notice the way I had spent my shoes in this video. I used them actually to create a symbolic masturbating with them. There is nothing vulgar in it; it is more to look at one's thoughts on the erotic universe.

This is the clip from the video from the political youth party

Dairy products!

There are many things you can use whipped cream, milk, and again it is only imagination, that puts a stop to this. If you are lacking inspiration, then you can get them from many different sources. Where you can borrow your inspiration from, may well be from films, plays, books, and advertising. The list is long, and remember, if it works somewhere else, then it could also be that it works for you in your strip show. Find out what is fascinating and so you can see if you cannot catch them in the same way. This is where you get to find out a little of what personal fantasies they may have. Where they have their fantasies and in which direction you can run it. It may take some time and some energy to figure this out on and remember it will probably pay off in the end. Then, you will have found the golden insights into what lies in your partners inner pleasure and fantasy.

I must have a rose for other interesting things!

Remember to end your show in a gallant manner, and one of the things all women like is to get roses, and this is where you will end by giving a rose, but it is not just women who like to be in the center. Most who love to be pampered will remember it. It has a magical effect on the majority of women who receive a rose. However, it is important that you save this rose slightly away, so she does not know what it is that it gets a little surprise for her. You can save it in a piece of cloth.

That way she does not know what it is, she is going to receive and play with her imagination and the idea of what it could be, she will receive. Moreover, remember as a child what effect a Christmas has on us, when we have not knowing what was inside, but could only guess at it.

Remember to end your show in a gallant manner, and one of the things all women like is to get roses, and this is where you will end by giving a rose, but it is not just women who like to be in the center. Most who love to be pampered will remember it. It has a magical effect on the majority of women who receive a rose. However, it is important that you save this rose slightly away, so she does not know what it is that it gets a little surprise for her. You can save it in a piece of cloth.

That is the point, it is like magic and the effect is on the person who comes out of it for when we come out of something where we are in unknown territory of our lives can make us insecure and that's the whole secret behind that you must use this technique. This will not have passed by us even if we become adults and are reminded to remember that we all like to be surprised.

Use your imagination in terms of props!

If you have any other ideas for something that can be used in your show, then try it again, it is only your own imagination, that holds you back and who says no to the ideas.

You are only as good as the proposals that I have made. The act is all about surprise and delight for them, that you have in mind to carry out your strip show. It could be it a closing in a bathtub, that just occurred to you inside or first place in met, there are many option and many things that you can use some of them are more fortunate than others. Again, it is as if I said only your own imagination and ideas, which set limits, for what could be interesting to include in your show. Again, remember to always respect, the others' boundaries, it should be fun for both of you, not just a fresh idea you have in your mind.

Chapter 5:How do I put a strip show together!

So now, we come to the fun part, and secure the part you want. How to start a strip show and how such shows are reviewed from start to finish. Yes, it is going to take some work by you, and yes, there is sure to be some part time in it, but if you choose to work out on the side, you'll want to rely on your diet. Again, it should all be up to you to find out what you have for skills and use them to the best of your abilities. Figure out what show you will be making, and make sure you have found the music you want to strip to.

You are therefore, actually ready to come to this part to get started with stripping. Whether you want to improvise or whether you make schematics to follow, is of course up to you but I will choose to make some plans for you here. So, you can get started in a fast and easy way. In addition, your show can be changed it if you need to. Whether you think there should be other things without going overboard and then you will have to change the whole concept.

I have decided to split it into three parts to make it easier for you. It can be daunting to think that one should start and then finally fail. So yes, I am willing do a little teaching on this point for you. For I am all right to use a little help at this point, to get you started but remember if you can do just that. I am forming all the things you need to use in your show to be made clear to you, so you can just continue. I have chosen to undergo a strip show as a gentleman, and I assume that it has three numbers of music on your CD as just ready to play and make your show alive.

Remember not to have socks on, this is a no go, because socks are not sexy on a man!

Part 1

When you start his or her show make sure the music is on and is running in the background, so you can get started with your strip show. You'll go and find your partner and get and make him or her sit in the chair. Then walk around them a few times, and as it happens, one can set the various props, so that person will come to see them. The ones that you will have in your show and later use them, on different times in the show. You start to take off your jacket; there are several ways that it can be taking off then by just normally taking it off, suffering tremendously, or as if you are about to make love to it. Depending on the person, you are stripping for and what you think is best for you and your show. It is about making it part of your show. Once you have thrown the jacket, you fall down in front of him or her, and start making an arm pulling whether to make them fast or slow is up to you.

Part 2

When the next track of the music you have selected is starting, you should be working on the next part of your strip show. It is going to take a little more enthusiasm and this is where you throw your shirt, you need a little time to unbutton or unzip it. You can always kneel before him or her, and slowly show a little more of your skin and obviously send them a look with your eyes. Remember, the eyes can also be used in the stripper show for you, and you may like to use your smile without it becoming too vigorous. Remember you are the sexy one in this whole situation so take it and utilize it. You can choose to have a T-shirt under the shirt, but a T-shirt is not necessary, and you have to be a little better than good if you want to use it on your show.

You might as well just have bare skin. Once you have thrown off your shirt and are standing bare-chested, you can choose to walk around, dance away from him or her, get hold of your water bottle, which you can use now. You take it and get on your knees. Begin to use it in an erotic way and end with pressing heavily in the middle so the water comes out of it, and let it come too high in the air and preferably at an angle so it hits you. Next, take the bottle and use it to pour it out all over you, in a seductive manner. Here it also came to your shoes also, you put them on her chair, between his or her thighs, and untie the laces. Then you take each shoe off and keep it, as it is approximately step height, one hand to hold the other sliding back and forth, once you've done with it just throw it away, but if you feel better just taking shoes off, take it and fold up so he or she can see your buttocks.

Part 3

Now you come to the last part of your show. You need to contend with your belt and it can also be removed in various ways. You can choose to pull it off, but you can also play around with it to pull it off in a slow manner. So now, you have only your pants on, you must pull them off and you can choose to walk around before you do it or just put your back to the person you have chosen to strip for. After bowing to your way of everything while you take hold of the coat, and in it you will come up again dragging your pants. Then you take hold of the bottle with the oil and go over and put yourself in a personal position then get someone to pour it over you, or else you pour it out on your skin and get him or her to rub on your body with their hands. Once it has been going on for a little piece of time, it is the time to finish your show. Get up, go over, and find the towel that you have saved the rose in, and it is important that you do not reveal what it is too early. However, play around with the thought that it could be anything, and only reveal it at the end that it is a rose that you ended with. It may be put in the mouth or taken in hand and then give it to him or her.

This was a fast way to go through a show, and you will get experience as you get more insights into the show and find out the things associated with it. You can let him or her touch your buttocks and spend more time on various other things, and how different things can be used. Yes, you can use candles to pour down on yourself, but it comes with experience in this respect. Good to like the attitude here from you.

Chapter 6: To get in shape through exercise!

To get in shape through exercise! There are many different training methods and ways to keep fit. You can strengthen and train with the things a fitness center contains, but you can also enjoy football, handball or just run fast a few times each week. It is not only one-way. You train on which is important for how the outcome will be. It is equally important that one choose to take time out, to run his or her strip show. In addition, yes, you are going to have to work out many times. Yes, it maybe you think you should just strip and only that. This is just one of the reasons, why you should practice a little on this. Because once you are in the situation, there are many things and thoughts that come into play, and yes you get nervous and might think you look silly.

Therefore, when you get the opportunity, set-aside some time to be trained. Your strip show in many ways is, and will be a repeat of many exercises. Moreover, find a time of day when you have time to practice, and yes, there you can easily spend over an hour on it. Yes, you can sometimes get tired of repeating the same exercise movements. Moreover, the music you use, if you choose it to be the same number, which will play until one gets tired of it. One of the things I learned in that period was to reward me, when I have done a show through a certain number of times. In this one way, you get bodies to think in a certain way, and this has a positive effect on the way you think, and causes the body to better remember. Moreover, yes this is only a proposal is not something you need to follow, if you can find your own way of doing it, it is just lovely in every way.

However, another thing is also you just need to remember is one's diet. It is incredibly important for you to get in shape. In addition, it to sleep at night and get over 8 hours' sleep. When it comes to getting in shape even though you practice the real program, to reach the finish will not succeed just as well as if you have had in mind. Having diet and sleep with mind throughout this process as training now time is all about. There are many ways to follow a diet plan on and I mention here is the only one among the many, as you will find out there on the market. So, choose one that you think might be particular to spend this time.

Remember this is only one of many cures you can choose, and remember in the last end you get freely receive many positive substances in the brain, which has a good and happy effect, on other things in your life and system. Here are some of them but I believe you know them one is dopamine and other endorphins. Some of the things you need to keep you from that do not have such a positive effect are the things I mention here though I think you know them. You've sure heard them in other contexts, but now I mention them again it's sugar, it's cool and it is alcohol as well as having bad effects on your body and yes, they are also used liberally by myself.

I know that most of us would like to live healthily but have the ability to fall into this self-destruction, it is quite natural that it is on the way. However, remember you must be aware of it, to know it is easier than done. Then again, remember to reward your body when you are going in the right direction, it can be to buy a book, a piece of clothing, or just something that you have really wanted for some time. Because when you reward your body and your entire system, you begin to think differently, and that is exactly what is it you want to get hold of in order to create change in your life. Not only that you will strip but also with everything in life and yes, you deserve it in every way.

Now what you could do, every time you get a craving for sugar, eat as much fruit as you take pleasure in. Moreover, yes, bananas. I recommend that you only eat for of few days. I know there is fruit sugar in it but to change the habits you have to start somewhere. You can start the day with muesli and some coffee or tea, depending on what you find to taste best. If you want something sweet in coffee, then take honey, and only a teaspoon, and yes, I did not like it at first but turned to it. If you must have milk, drink it as semi-skimmed milk. You need to keep yourself from red meat and as much as possible you eat chicken or fish. Oh, yes, once in a week it is ok with red meat such as beef or pork, this is something that is hard to break down in the body. When you get your evening meal, eat as many vegetables as possible, for lunch and bread without butter or other products in the same style.

When you are training, it is important that you get yourself up on that level where you feel a life and feel your exercise. Get your heart rate up there where you can feel it for your entire system. The use of 30 minutes every time you exercise and even see if you cannot get your PMB being 90 or high at all time, and that it will lie all the time during your workout, and yes, the start it is hard and difficult but after hand as the body gets started turning on to it.

Chapter 7: My time as a stripper!

There are so many stories to my time as a stripper, and I will mention some of them here. And yes, some of them, are weird while others are fun. I want to share some of them as I write to you about my life as a stripper. I hope you get some pleasure out of it you read these stories, and yes there are certain parts I have not mentioned, because I cannot remember every single show I have made. There are many stories and many times I was off stripping 4 to 6 times in an evening, although it was not often. However it happened, and at the same time, I enjoyed myself with the things I shared. The experiences I got under way in all ways has enriched me as the person I am. I always want to say thanks to the people I have been out and stripping for. They were both sweet and kind ordinary people as well in all ways. Some of them remember I still like to charm, and be good-looking. I hope you will enjoy what you read.

I myself worked in this area as a stripper, and have worked both in Denmark and in Sweden and did work for one of the biggest companies all over. I also went stripping in Germany, although it only for a short time but it was still a good adventure to get the experience. Therefore, I know what thoughts and emotions are going through the mind, when you stand in the position of having to throw ones' clothes to the wind. For indeed it exceeds its limit in every way, and it also provides a huge adrenalin kick to complete the experience. To do something where you come out on shaky ground in your own perception.

How to start it that you choose to take this option like this, and start a career as a stripper. Yes, it is a good question. I was still part time but, on my way. I was both stripper and a bartender. I believe there were many things that came into play when I stopped and I took this choice. Equally well it was easy when I think back of how and why I chose my selections. As changes happen in your life, there are many ways but also the experiences. What I got out of it was not stripping for the money and there were some consequences of my choices. When choosing a profession as a stripper and having a mate at home, as well as working with one, one of them is going to be comparing. When a relationship is based on the early, it requires a lot from both sides.

Had you asked me at age 20, if I would have chosen to be a stripper, I probably would have looked at you very strange. However, when I started as a stripper, I was just getting out of a 30-year relationship and stood alone. I was in a place in my life where I wanted to try many new things. I had just gone out of a relationship and now stood the fact that I had the freedom to do what wanted with my life, without having to worry about my old partner who was in my life. This freedom led me in this direction both because I wanted to test myself in a new and different way, and because I was curious, about life and what it might have to offer. Again, how could it be that I just took these selections? You think about it and I'll try to be as honest as I can about giving you a reasonable answer.

However, as I said, then I started stripping when I was 30 years old, and I kept stripping for the next 6 years. However, I think I was in a period of my life where I wanted to test myself and to check my own limits. I think it was best happening in these selections as a stripper, and had enough of a performance that was different from what reality was. Sometimes it was nice to be able to be enriched, in this way with how the reality really looked. However, one of the things that caught me, and made me go to this, was the thought that it would be easy to score women and it was lucrative with the money move too. Therefore, I think it was a good combination of selections.

I still remember my first show, it went in Flensburg by an erotic fair and I particularly remember a week in advance. Having been in contact with Preben from the stripper king's girls and he wanted to invite me to strip. This was both to see if I had what it required to implement being a stripper. I can remember that I have had put some music together for my show, and that I nodded to DJ who smiled and went towards it. He had been told it was my first show, and that I have never done this before. He was pretty nice and told to all that they should take it easy with me, as this was the first time I had to strip.

Yes, it was an incredibly poor show in every way and I was nervous and unsure. I still remember when I was in the middle of the show when this thought came, 'what am I doing here?' And I just felt that uncertainty slowly but surely slipping forward and becoming more on edge than I could have imagined. After I had completed my show, I got a huge applause from the audience who were present. Many had chosen to leave. This was probably because I was new, and also, the worst stripper show in history. I was left with a great feeling that was difficult to describe but I stayed high for this. And I can remember that I thought if I could get approved for this, I might also be able to make a living for me in this world. For the rest of the Erotica World, I opted to look at the male strippers and look at how their shows defined them. I thought I had a lot to learn but I loved to take the chance.

20 days later I was invited to DM in Male Strip. Inside then, I had done a lot on the account like they wanted me to be taking sun, and much of it and getting rid of a lot of hair on the whole body, for I have learned from the male strippers it was part of the game of being a stripper. I had gotten much more out of my training and had come into the form they wanted me to be in. I chose to take a lot of sun in the form of Solaria. I also spent a lot of time and energy in my strip show and having made a kung Fu strip. Today, I probably would have done something else, but I did not see so much about the things women smiled about and found sexy. However, there was one thing I had chosen to include in my show and I continued to use it. It was to give a rose at the end of my show. Actually, it was to a woman I was

sitting with at the Erotic event. As she recommended me to do it and since then, this was one of the things that has followed me on my way as a stripper. To join my show of how to dispose of a red rose for the woman who was selected. As I should have experienced, it has a very positive effect on the woman who is the sacrifice. Perhaps sacrifice is not the right word but her which gets the experience.

There were 8 people who participated in DM not thinking it was so many, so it was an experience. I heard a lot robber stories from amongst many of the strippers. Not that I got a special space but I attended it. Shortly after this was the championships strip and I got my first strip show in Aarhus. I kept practicing and going through my show all the time so I finally could remember everything that was going to happen. I started to do the show and I had only the one show. I remember when arrived, I have persuaded a friend of mine to go along because I was nervous. I was delighted that I should be allowed to act and strip at the same time for money. We played pool to waste the time before I had to go onto stage. I believe there were 15 people they looked at me the first time I appeared. Yes, there was a woman who looked like she wanted something more than just talk, but I was too nervous to do anything about it. Shortly after I was done, we took off again. I remember I was quite high about it and had lot of energy in the body. I could sure be running throughout the home from Aarhus, which was the feeling I did feel and at the same time, I was very high on this feeling.

I was proud that it had succeeded and shortly after that, I found out I should strip in Aabenraa (Town in Denmark), on one of the local sites. It was to be a full house since it was not very often that there would be a strip at many of these locations. So, I had become a draw for the bright eyes and yes, I have in that time made two shows. I worked on being better than I have been before. I made a great show of one of the most beautiful women in the area. I can remember her name. Mette. And that I probably would not have come in contact with her if, I had not stripped for her. However, we talked briefly together and had a little contact with her for a while after I had gone to Copenhagen. I remember that she was an incredibly beautiful and charming woman.

It was shortly before I moved to Copenhagen. One show in Germany was in Flensburg. It was a 25-year birthday and was always held at the same time each year. There were eight guests and yes, they were sweet. I talked with the guests afterwards although it was hard, since I was not particularly strong in German and selected quick to go back home to Denmark again. However, I do remember that she was absolutely delighted to receive the rose that I always finish my show with. I made it through the 6 years as I was a part of the entertainment.

Just when I moved to Copenhagen, I met a woman who did not go very long before I came into a relationship with her and then I did stop to strip. The relationship held for only eight months, and then I could feel that I was not finished stripping. So soon after, I returned to this environment and started full-blown. And the first show I got then was in Roskilde on a bodega where I was to strip with another stripper, and has made me a moving party strip and then I started to run in the positions to be more thorough in my life for stripping.

After the hand, I came across more and more event companies like 'garden' with strip here, including the Danish show service, 'stripper queen' and the Swedish strip companies. Just to name some of them I ran into and became employed by for performing strip shows around the country. I and also came over to the other side of the strait for stripping. Looks like I have done many stripping shows and cannot remember them all. But I will mention some of them have been quite different, and actually funny to think back on in this time of my life.

Now I just began telling my experiences because I have a part, and it is not all I can remember when they come and happen. I know there are many of them, and I'll try to get them as well for it is a little funny or a little weird at this point. So, I'll throw myself just out of this and then just tell you what I can for I cannot really remember. When the various strip shows passed on... (there were many of them) ...and it was incredibly fun in all ways. That is how life is sometimes. However, having said that, it was a fun time but with many experiences.

I know it's nice that people hit on you and want you as the person you are, that's a given and it feels good to experience this from another human being. Seems to have ended with a deliciousness or you are able to attract another person. In addition, I am pretty surprised, when I go out and do a strip show in a nursing home for a woman of 90 years. It was her grandson, who had ordered a strip, and it was to be a firefighter, for she really loved firemen even if she was a little demented as this could really get her out of the chair. It was a Friday, I had gotten this show and it was at Frederiksberg. I had to talk to her grandson the day before, I had to act and I wanted to know a little about what it was I was getting into. And I got just an ordinary knowledge about how she loves men and was especially happy about firemen, and she would love to have this done for her. I could come and be stripping as a firefighter for her. This would be her greatest wish.

I made ready to come out for this birthday celebration, with her whole family and when I arrived at the nursing home, I was greeted by a sweet and gracious person from the staff, who was kind enough to guide me in the direction of the place where there was to be the birthday celebration. I met the grandson that I just talked with and he thought it was cool that I would give her this experience. I said that I usually only have 18 to 25 year old birthday girls, so it was nice to get a different experience this time. I started the show when the whole family gathered. She sat and smiled and was happy for this experience. When I was done with my show. I was asked if I could imagine a bite to eat with them and if I would like to do this. I graciously accepted.

When I sat at the table, I was allowed to sit next to the elderly birthday woman. She was at the head of the table and they were enjoying themselves but I did not count that something was to take place and that I would be probably be a little surprised about it. For while I was sitting here I felt a hand on my knee. It was the older woman who seems that she wanted a little attention. I pushed her hand away three times and became a little beside myself. She tried again but in a different way. She asked if I could not scratch her on her back this time I had no problem with this. But, then she asked if I could not scratch her legs. I smiled and politely said no thanks with a smile on my lips. Her family started laughing because they could see that I was a little beside myself. I have never tried to be with a woman of 90 who had tempted me but this one time was going to be the only time.

I was going to Helsingør, (Town in Denmark) and do a strip show. I cannot but smile but I will get to that. I had finished working and got off of work late. Then it was off to Elsinore to make a show and I remember that the place was called '**Emma**'. However, I am not sure if it was called something more than that, but I had to do a show up there and was told that there it was lady's Night. As there was to be about 30 to 40 women in this place, I went through locally and dropped some glances in my direction. They had already shown who I was and what was needed. There were some young men as waiters in bare torsos and socializing around these women, to get them to have a good night. I met the owner of the site and was quickly talking to her about, how I should dress on and the normal information. I wanted to know as to when to do my strip show.

Before I start to do my show, I try to get around to many of the guest as possible, so that all are allowed to have a small part of the strip show personalized. I would have to purchase a large box of folded roses so I could share a little around to the various women who were present, there were 13 roses in all, so there were 13 women who were special like that night. When I was finished, I stood up at the bar and enjoyed a soft drink and relaxed. There was a part of me soaking up all the praise and yes, I love praise. It is a nice feeling to experience that others actually like what you do also it's strip-worthy. As I stood there and enjoyed my water before I would go back, there came a woman up to me. One of the things I very fast noticed was her huge breasts, probably because she was a very thin woman at the same time. It was probably the wobbling as to her breasts came to see so violently, for she was an otherwise ordinary-looking woman. However, she came over to me, and said that she would give me 5000 kr, to strip for her. I believe in the first instance the act that I should strip, but it is about that she would buy me for sex for one night.

Yes, I could have said yes, but I was told that I was a stripper and not to run an Escort, and was therefore not interested in taking up this offer but I thanked her nicely for this offer. I chose to drink out and then figure out how to get home to Amager again. It is always nice to experience that others find a change that they actually are will to pay money, to enjoy one's body, but I think I just do not. I would not feel good about myself. I could have said yes but I have a great respect towards others that can do this. Consecutively, I worked to tell others to strip and that an Escort was not the same. So, if I had said yes to this, I would probably feel it would have been morally wrong. It is not as good for any type of people. I would not have agreed to have sex with someone, if it had come into this.

A year later, I was in Hvidovre (Town in Denmark) to strip and on that occasion, I met one of the boys who had been up to discuss 'Emma' and serve for the evening and it was fun to talk to him. This came from that he thought he had seen another strip show as like my strip show, and when I asked him how it was he told me, that he would have been a waiter in the place called 'Emma'. I talked shortly after my show and I would have to pass, that night, to another show.

69

Have you ever tried as a man to be sold as a date? I must also tell the next stripper story. I remember a friend of mine called and told me that he was missing some of his wait staff and needed a bare-chested server and sure enough I was one. I just had to be on for 2 hours and comforting customers. I went in there and the place was in Nørreport (Town part in Copenhagen) this place was called 'Jagtstuen', where they have the Lady's Night. I entered the site and was to be just bare-chested, and a server for the various women. They were aged 18-45 years and having good time in it and enjoy themselves. After the stripper have been on was that really started it and the women were keen on seeing meat so it ended up with the two young men who were present and had to sell a new product from Carlsberg.

After they have stood there collectively when I began to ask them who they were, and what they did for a living and if they were single, as well as some other issues, which are now once in used in a conversation. When I had the information that could make the night a more fun, I sought out the women, who stood for this event, and asked the young men to stand in bare-chested. Yes, I think she should ask all women about it and it happened so and ended up they stood in bare-chested, and walked no laps after some time. I turned back to the young lady who stood for the event, and asked if she have seen coyote ugly, and have her for my luck then told me that one of the guys were single, and if we should sell him as a date for these women. Yes, as I said so happened that the young man got sold for 850 kr.- and for the money he would invite the woman out and search for that she got a good night.

***

Sometimes I may well come to wonder about people. I have been out and making two strip shows. Where I have had one of my stand-up comedian friends He did not have many gigs so I thought he should have this opportunity to do so. However, when I have a show back he would like to go home to his wife, and socialize so I put him in Valby where he resides. I went in for my next show, which should be out in Nørrebro, and it was a 21st birthday. I was climbing the stairs when her brother stopped me; he looks me deep in the eyes and then asks, "if I pay something extra, can you fuck my sister?" I got pretty surprised about this, I've never actually met anyone like this with their sister, to have sex with a stranger and then pay for it. I answered as I have always done that I did not have sex with anyone for money. The brother gave me a little extra, secure in the hope that I would change my mind, and I thought his sister was unlucky to look at or if there was anything that was wrong with her. Actually, she was a very pretty woman and yes, she was pushy, but it follows the course of this profession I got stripping and ate together with them. Some incredibly nice people.

Sometimes, some people remember many of the things they have made over time. I stood at a bar in the town and was drunk. Four women came over to me and asked if I was not a stripper named Lars and to this I answered yes. They could remember my show and we talked a little bit together, I asked how long ago it was since I stripped for them, and they told me that it was 4 years ago. I got a little surprised and thought, that there was not so much going on in their lives or else it was a really good show, and yes, it's then up to the individual to judge. It is a little funny to think that you may be able to imprint upon others this way and that.

***

Sometime you will encounter a well-known person. I had after having been dealt some experiences when I met with respect to her with stripping. I was asked to go to North Sjælland and do a strip show. When I was finished, there was one of the guests who seemed familiar. I could not put into words who it was or where I knew her from. I asked around a bit and the other guests told me that her name was Julia. Then it dawned on me that it was Julia from a band. (Blue eyes) I was young when I had been a fan of her and her band. I could not let go and had to ask for an autograph from her. And I got it from her and gave her a thank you for it and the experience.

The best day of my life, sometimes is to get others to affect one another in some very positive ways. I have experienced this many times that I apparently have been able to influence people around me, but I do not think much about it. However, I am always about other people's joy and happiness even if I do not get the same experience. It could be when my friends or girlfriends come over so I am on their way. Seems of course that it is nice with happiness in our lives, but only with the history of this element. I was just starting in the Swedish strip company, and had gotten my first job so, I was going to be doing a strip show in Sweden.

It was over in Malmø (Town in Sweden) and it was just to jump into the car and go, I came in one of my variety show outfits, but I did not know was the fact that she always had dreamed to have this experience, and it was her imagination coming to life through the show I made for her. Afterwards, when I was about to go, I can still remember the words she said to me, "I get touched by these words, which in many ways had the effect on the other. It has the best days of my life." But I told her that it was when she got married, to come with her husband. She was quite touched to tears and told me yes. It gives me joy to have given another human joy on the way for I can think of nothing better.

***

Sometimes when you become a year older, you can

get your wish fulfilled for your birthday. I still remember when I was called by a Danish show service who had a job for me. I had to go out and strip for a 16-year-old girl's birthday. I had gotten the number from the girl's father, and went and had a chat with him about what was going to happen. I told how what would happen in the show and I emphasized that I in no way, would I go over his limits. The father told me that since they had been inside and looking around, his daughter expressed that I was the hottest stripper, and it is always nice to get those words on your way in life. I think it is rewarding to experience this even if it was a 90-year or 16 year old so it is always nice and yes thank you for the experiences.

In Sweden, I had dressed and went ahead with the show, the other strippers were very nervous, but this probably had something to do with their age. Such was the case throughout the show that they were nervous and equally well their muscles seemed to be tightening. It is probably something to do with the hormones driving around in the bodies at that age. I concluded my acts by disposing of the roses to all those who were singled out by me earlier. But there came an extra girl and she had taken her boyfriend. So, I mentioned that he indeed had been the real part of what a rose could lead to. I thanked him and went next door and they went wild in a form of praise of joy. And they cried when Will, (the next stripper) could not do anything but to smile at the phrase.

Those in the municipality must of course also have some fun. I got a call from Danish show service who had a job to do. As always, I was keen on getting out and stripping. I heard it was for the Copenhagen municipality, in their department of social services for the elderly. I could not help but smile a part of the time. I worked even in the older areas and I helped other people who needed various kinds of help. There was a 50-year birthday for a woman and she had Christmas lights in the eyes. And as always, I concluded with a rose to please the woman. After the show I sat a bit and talked to her and when she heard that I worked inside for elderly care, it became very spontaneous that she was pleased to be old. Some things, we as human beings, will always look forward to in life.

Sometimes you can get into a movie. Yes, I have actually been in a movie or at least, my two nuts are in a movie called 'Klassefesten Class Party'. They wanted to use some male nuts in a stand in the nuts scene in the film. I was contact by the Danish show service. I received a stripping job through them and they called me because they had a special job for me, and here they told me about the job. They said to me it would mean that my nuts were to be in a Danish play movie. And I could not help but thank them and say yes to the opportunity. At the same time it was funny to experience this.

TRIUMPH

Klubblad nr. 3 2014 MC Owners Club Denmark

Læs i dette nummer om:

- Toldsyn
- Sommerens træf.
- Generalforsamlingen.
- Studietur til England.
- Isle of Møn.
- United MC´s 25 års jubilæum
- Kristians Triumph 900T 300
- Knutte og Flemmings historie

Og meget, meget mere.

God fornøjelse.

Se mere på:

www.triumphmc.dk

Forsidebillede: Ejer Michael Lyngberg, Rønne.

It ended up that I made in an MC leave the 'Danish Triumph', and I had taken the cover page of the magazine, in which number I was in, and texted for what they wrote about me in the paper. The text was: "For such a party, shall meet many different and fun people. Here is Lars, Lars was a photographer for the party. And I have seen his nuts and you have also if you have seen the sauna scene in the film, "Class Party number 1."

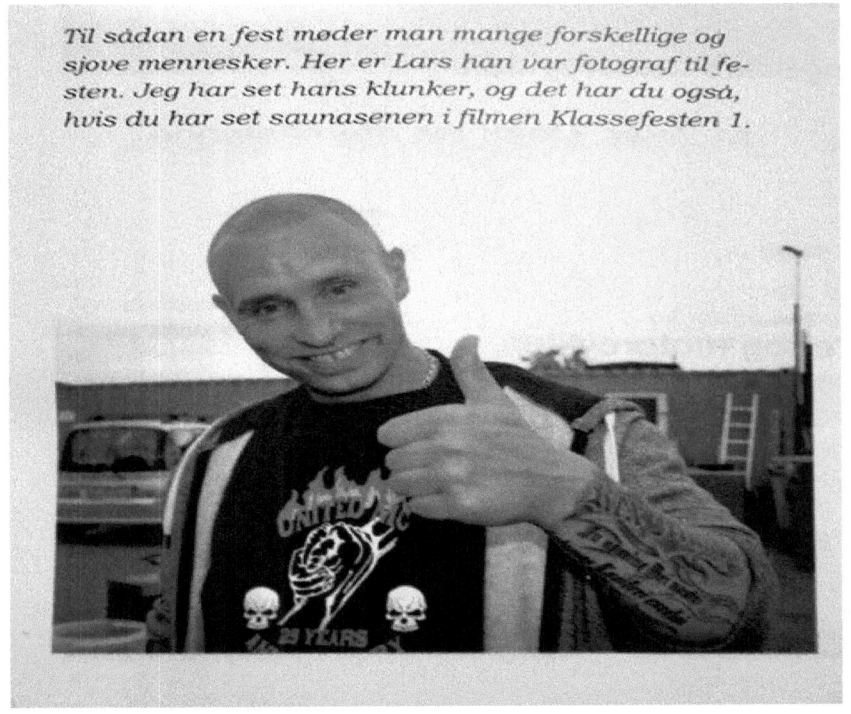

Til sådan en fest møder man mange forskellige og sjove mennesker. Her er Lars han var fotograf til festen. Jeg har set hans klunker, og det har du også, hvis du har set saunasenen i filmen Klassefesten 1.

I have some other stories but I think I have come up with enough of them here. I hope you have rejoiced over them or got a smile from them.

Chapter 8: What men do brazenly and what makes women smile!

I have asked some questions of some of the acquaintances I have come across through the years. The questions which I think would be interesting to let you read and gain insights into. Yes, I know that women differ in what turns them on and what they find sexy. I have a great respect for the women who chose to participate and many thanks to you for your answers, which I greatly appreciate. For the part of, 'the art of stripping' is to the charm and makes a woman feel appreciated on a very special way. Therefore, I have made some questions that I think could, and can be of help.

I have chosen to follow the same series of questions to ask different people. As you will see farther down. I have specifically chosen to have many different types of people in different ages. However, this is just to give you an idea and a helping hand at this point. For even if you as a man get it wrong, you can still give the women you choose a good and enriched experience.

Remember we all like to be in the center and enjoying the attention in our life. I have found that it is like this in every situation whether it is first time we meet another person or whether it's over a dinner. At parties or other situations where people are present, all will enjoy being the one who is in the center. This also applies when you choose to strip for one. Remember, the woman can do it for you if you like it. So, learn this and give her this experience.

All the different people I asked have been in different ages ranging from 18 to 50. It's a wide mix and there are many different types of people who have all had their opinions on what they think of my questions. Some of them liked the idea of a man who strips and others did not like them. The people are from many different environments, and there is also a politician. There is a political asset stripper, a former porn actor and people in all ends of the society have responded.

I have also decided to ask gay men what turns them on because I think that it is also important to get more aspects of what it is that makes a human more sexually desirable. There are some things that, capture our way of looking at another person and, sexily thinking that this person is truly beautiful in every way.

A. What do you find sexy in a man!

B. What part of a man do you gaze at first when you see him for the first time!

C. How can you be a sexy woman without him touching you!

D. Which part of man you find most sexy!

E. Can a contact be enough to awaken something in you (not an intimate place of your body)!

F. How do you like to be surprised!

G. What fantasy would you rather see a man strip as!

H. What causes you to lose focus from a man? What he must do or say!

I. If a man should deliver a gift or flowers, how do you think it could be a little more interesting if it was possible for you!

J. How can a man seduce you and make you feel comfortable in his company!

Here is the answer to my questions as I asked, Christine.

A. What do you find sexy in a man?

When a man is in cheeky the first place with all his charisma / attitude. It is also the first thing you notice until the small details emerge. Personally, an important role to play is when it is said that a woman cannot help but look for the "smaller" things. Hands, eyes, smile and charm is what I find most attractive in a man.

B. What part of a man do you gaze at first when you see him for the first time!

Most sexy is a man's hands, ass and eyes.

C. How can you be a sexy woman without him touching you!

One knows that you can be sexy without touching one by sending a couple of flirty eyes, and a jauntily smile, it also shows he is interested in getting the woman.

D. Which part of man you find most sexy?

Most sexy is in a man's hands, ass and eyes.

E. Can a contact be enough to awaken something in you (not an intimate place of your body)?

It depends on whether one is interested in the person, if one does not have the attraction to him, a touch will not awaken anything. However, if one has an attraction, a contact for example on the cheek, would be enough.

F. How do you like to be surprised?

Like to be surprised with such a good dinner, that you can see he really made it count, or lit candles everywhere to create a nice, cozy atmosphere.

G. What fantasy would you rather see a man strip as?

The cheeky strip one can get from a man is when it is spontaneously for the woman, but possibly something he has planned

H. What causes you to lose focus from a man? What he must do or say!

If he is arrogant, or demeaning towards you, you lose focus quickly. If you are a couple with one, it may be that he expects the woman to do it all and never appreciate the things you do for him.

I. If a man shall deliver a gift or flowers, how to think it could be a little more interesting if it is possible to you!

It could be, for instance, doing something together and you suddenly got flowers and some sweet words to you. Instead of one who always just receives something and a kiss, and that's it.

J. How can a man seduce you and make you feel comfortable in his company!

He should be humorous and rest well in itself, a man who exudes too much uncertainty is not for me. He must be able to make me smile, laugh, and feel good - first that he can seduce the example. To show he is very interested in inquiring into one caress is also important.

***

Here is the answer to my questions as I asked for Liselott. She wanted to have an additional question answered.

A. What do you find sexy in a man?

The way she dresses and behaves. The whole human.

B. What part of a man do you gaze at first when you see him for the first time!

His eyes are what I caught the first, they reflect to me a lot.

C. How can you be a sexy woman without him touching you!

A glance, a gesture, gentleman.

D. Which part of man you find most sexy?

his mouth

E. Can a contact be enough to awaken something in you (not an intimate place of your body)?

Certainly, the Right Man teeth sparks at the mere touch no matter where it is.

F. How do you like to be surprised?

A spontaneous picnic, come home after work and example, he has covered up on the floor with some delicious,

G. What fantasy would you rather see a man strip as?

A man in uniform always takes cones, be pilot, fireman ect

H. What causes you to lose focus from a man? What he must do or say!

Fart, burp, smack is very charmless.

I. If a man shall deliver a gift or flowers, how to think it could be a little more interesting if it is possible to you?

As a surprise one day you do not expect it.

J. How can a man seduce you and make you feel comfortable in his company?

Being MAN, book a table somewhere he has appointed, commissioned the best secluded table in the room, and have agreed on food and drinks with the staff to give me, a sensual experience and good fun.

What is the worst he can do so you may not be deceived?

Let me order from a menu and every time I ask him what he wants he says, "I don't know…what do you want?"

***

Here is the answer to my questions as I asked for Susan

A. What do you find sexy in a man?

Frankly, I do not think there is anything particularly sexy about a man.

B. What part of a man do you gaze at first when you see him for the first time!

His eyes - you can see various eyes.

C. How can you be a sexy woman without him touching you!

A look - yes, the eyes means a lot to me.

D. Which part of man you find most sexy?

If not, I must say his eyes again, otherwise hands. It should certainly not be soft office hands.

E. Can a contact be enough to awaken something in you (not an intimate place of your body)?

It can certainly - an arm around the shoulder, a touch of the hair on a cheek and a gentle kiss (not necessarily at the mouth)

F. How do you like to be surprised?

A kiss on the neck, a touch of cheek, a flower

G. What fantasy would you rather see a man strip as?

I'm probably boring; but that kind cannot turn me

H. What causes you to lose focus from a man? What he must do or say!

Vulgar behavior, rough approximations and words.

I. If a man shall deliver a gift or flowers, how to think it could be a little more interesting if it is possible to you?

It could be fun, he focuses on the eyes and brings me, where the gift is and remove your hands from my eyes - I have never tried.

J. How can a man seduce you and make you feel comfortable in his company?

By inviting me out - not necessarily at dinner; but just for a walk. By keeping my hand - and most importantly: Being able to be silent with me.

***

Here is the answer to my questions as I asked for Camilla

A. What do you find sexy in a man?

His smile. There is nothing better than to see a guy smile sweet, sexiness or loving.

B. What part of a man do you gaze at first when you see him for the first time!

His charisma. It is the whole that I see first.

C. How can you be a sexy woman without him touching you!

By resting in themselves and have the interests of the experience.

D. Which part of man you find most sexy?

Hands and upper body

E. Can a contact be enough to awaken something in you (not an intimate place of your body)?

Definitely! Sometimes more than the direct places. The excitement passing through the heart. At least with me.

F. How do you like to be surprised?

When he does something, I just did not expect, or which are normally not him, but do it because he knows that it means a lot to me. It is certainly not the size of the surprise, but more thought behind it.

G. What fantasy would you rather see a man strip as?

No idea.

H. What causes you to lose focus from a man? What he must do or say!

If he becomes too intrusive in a bad way. Says a bunch of crap or acts sort of desperate.

I. If a man shall deliver a gift or flowers, how to think it could be a little more interesting if it is possible to you?

I do not know.

J. How can a man seduce you and make you feel comfortable in his company?

Have humor and be themselves. Not make a lot of artificial crap to impress me. It just has to be real.

***

Here is the answer to my questions as I asked a woman who wanted to remain anonymous. and that is fine with me, and here come her lovely responses.

A. What do you find sexy in a man?

It is now a little sketchy, but if a man goes in suits (and feels comfortable in them), I am sold on site. There are (almost) none of which is more than the bold.

B. What part of a man do you gaze at first when you see him for the first time!

Hmm... It must be his charisma. I do not go for looks, but more whether he is confident, fashionable and so on. Also, if he has a sweet smile.

C. How can you be a sexy woman without him touching you!

Honestly, I know not. I have some things in the luggage that makes I do not particularly be very good in relationships with sex, and being intimate with someone other than myself, and not even that it goes very well. However, I practice and go as forward as quietly. However, it requires that I am first 100% comfortable with the person I should be with.

D. Which part of man you find most sexy?

First, I would write that I did not know it, but when I now think of it, I have come forward to it must be his smile. It must be like to be a little sexy, sensual. Like it as a grandmother would call for a hotti. Moreover, if your eyes saw rays while I am completely gone.

E. Can a contact be enough to awaken something in you (not an intimate place of your body)?

It depends on how you think the question. A conservative lovingly strokes on the forearm or a breath in the neck can easily awaken something in me. It need not always be sexually, but just the feeling of security and love.

F. How do you like to be surprised?

At this point, I got no answer

G. What fantasy would you rather see a man strip as?

I cannot answer.

H. What causes you to lose focus from a man? What he

must do or say!

I can be good and irritated and lose focus, if a man is too unsure of himself and his actions. Believe little more on yourself and you want me too. You definitely do not need to be a macho man, but a man who always apologizes for even the smallest and most insignificant things can probably turn me off.

I. If a man shall deliver a gift or flowers, how to think it could be a little more interesting if it is possible to you?

Now I am personally in a relationship where I gradually is on first name terms with the bid from the local flower trade, and I think that it is a little nice that there will be another person with something to me. The boyfriend is a seaman and therefore away for a long period of time and therefore arouses a little in me when a bunch of flowers, as it is one of the only ways he can do something physical for me when he's gone. If I am tired and sad that he is gone, disappearing all the thoughts with a bouquet of flowers, and it sounds so simply and it is perhaps too. Just not for me.

J. How can a man seduce you and make you feel comfortable in his company?

If a man seduces me, he will include some of all of the above. He must be loving, make me feel like the only girl in the world, show his feelings and not be cold as many men unfortunately are. He must be gallant and well dressed. Be a nice man for life, but a beast to party (I did not say!) He just has to be true to myself, and all else will be enough by itself.

***

Here is the answer to my questions as I asked for Grethe

    A. What do you find sexy in a man?

A good ass, beautiful eyes, tattoos

    B. What part of a man do you gaze at first when you see him for the first time!

Eyes, smile and body

    C. How can you be a sexy woman without him touching you!

Scent, charisma

    D. Which part of man you find most sexy?

Ass and dick

    E. Can a contact be enough to awaken something in you (not an intimate place of your body)?

Yes certainly, kiss on the neck

F. How do you like to be surprised?

Naughty text messages, he takes control

G. What fantasy would you rather see a man strip as?

In uniform. (police or military

H. What causes you to lose focus from a man? What he must do or say!

Lying or in fidelity

I. If a man should deliver a gift or flowers, how do you think it could be a little more interesting if it was possible for you!

Opposite me, very seductive / flirty

J. How can a man seduce you and make you feel comfortable in his company!

Take control, kiss, exploratory fingers

97

Here is the answer to my questions as I asked for Pia

A. What do you find sexy in a man?

I think it is a combination of many things, is naughty by a man. He should not just look good, or be well built, but there must be something in the way he looks at one on. That, he says, are allowed to have an extra glow, both in the way it is said, and what he says.

B. What part of a man do you gaze at first when you see him for the first time!

I think it is his face.

C. How can you be a sexy woman without him touching you!

A man can be sexy by the way he behaves. The way he says and does things. There are small secret messages without saying so directly.

D. Which part of man you find most sexy?

I think the man's hands are sexy.

E. Can a contact be enough to awaken something in you (not an intimate place of your body)?

Oh ...... there are definitely places you can touch and awaken everything good in me.

F. How do you like to be surprised?

Child-free. Adult time, out of the house. Hands on the body, and does not like intimate places.

G. What fantasy would you rather see a man strip as?

I do not think stripping men are delicious.

H. What causes you to lose focus from a man what he must do or say?

Monotony.

I. If a man shall deliver a gift or flowers, how to think it could be a little more interesting if it is possible to you?

If I am even without the child. We might. Not at home and we have the opportunity to be together undisturbed without electric media. Then we can focus on each other. However, a bouquet of flowers is always nice with a kiss.

J. How can a man seduce you and make you feel comfortable in his company?

Ha ha. Here I can as well be a bit unconventional, because I like it hard. Turns us at each other and know each other, can a wild assault with a little "forced sex" always be good. Otherwise, he just cuddle the tips of my hair, scratching me lightly between the shoulder blades and neck ... grrrr ....

***

Here is the answer to my questions as I asked for Maria

A. What do you find sexy in a man?

The eyes are important to me. They need to radiate heat and intense, so you are drawn to them.

B. What part of a man do you gaze at first when you see him for the first time!

Again, the eyes and hands of the sexy in a man.

C. How can you be a sexy woman without him touching you!

He needs to radiate heat and be intense, so you are drawn to him.

D. Which part of man you find most sexy?

Again, the eyes and hands of the sexiest in a man.

E. Can a contact be enough to awaken something in you (not an intimate place of your body)?

I like to be cuddled in the neck, being stroked on his hands and a special place behind the knees

F. How do you like to be surprised?

I think that surprises are wonderful - as long as it is not surprise parties! It can be anything from a home-picked bouquet of flowers for a spontaneous dinner in town. A bath with scented oils, to expect after a long working day or a DVD evening on the couch with a movie, we did not get to see the movies.

G. What fantasy would you rather see a man strip as?

My Boyfriend works within the Italian military police, and is mega hot in his uniform -so one uniform -strip is perfect!

H. What causes you to lose focus from a man what he must do or say?

Men must be honest. I hate insincerity and would rather have the truth. Jealousy is ok - but I will not be controlled and will not report.

I. If a man shall deliver a gift or flowers, how to think it could be a little more interesting if it is possible to you?

I love wild flowers - the others would call weeds. A bouquet picked in a field, or in a ditch makes, mega great joy to me.

J. How can a man seduce you and make you feel

comfortable in his company?

Gifts from the heart. It does not have to be an expensive thing - it may well be a book I want to read, as suddenly lie on my night table to seduce me I shall know him. I will turn on him and see that he turns to me. There must be sparks in the air; he must look intently at me and without words say everything with the eyes. He must be able to make me laugh - MUCH - be smart, be able to leave his mobile fit into your pocket instead of check messages and respond while we are together on a restaurant.

***

Here is the answer to my questions as I asked for Karina

A. What do you find sexy in a man?

His brain. But it requires that I know him really well, because there also with the brain hears trust, sharing intimate details of life, dreams, hope etc. as sharing intimate details that turns both of us and which we can build on.

B. What part of a man do you gaze at first when you see him for the first time!

It depends on whether it is an unknown man I did not get to know, so it does not take much, but the radiation, way to move on, a smile, a twinkle in the eye or mere a go ass. However, he must catch my interest more than just a look at a good ass and a cheeky smile - there must brain and a conversation of this kind do not really stop again but goes on day after day and catches me and him.

C. How can you be a sexy woman without him touching you!

By being himself, not have any great need to prove anything to anyone, be self ... and could have a conversation about his interests without becoming a monologue, but how he does it interest him alive for one, listening and asking, but even for the opportunity to speak. Then have some things you may be interested in together and separately, without necessarily agreeing or do it at the same time and in the same way - it would rather not become common camping suit and synchronous Living.

D. Which part of man you find most sexy?

So absolutely brain. Being allowed to be let into a man's thought universe is sexy. Then glances and hands.... In addition, the rest of him.

E. Can a contact be enough to awaken something in you (not an intimate place of your body)?

Yes example. His hand being laid on my neck when we wash up, then I become soft and warm inside.

F. How do you like to be surprised?

I like many ways. Many small surprises every day, whether it is "just" a kiss or caress, when I just recorded something that he shares his day, has a few good beers with home etc...

G. What fantasy would you rather see a man strip as?

My boyfriend.

H. What causes you to lose focus from a man what he must do or say?

As in losing interest? That he is too demanding, too unsure of himself, using me and the other as crutches to stiff a poor self-esteem of at humiliate and belittle me /others. Or he makes me lose focus on what I've been doing, because he makes me weak in the knees and the brain of anything he does? In order to be so not so much for a hand in the neck and then a wink followed by that look, I am to curl up ... and my boyfriend knows when he has lured me.

I. If a man shall deliver a gift or flowers, how to think it could be a little more interesting if it is possible to you?

It is unexpected. So, it's pretty much irrelevant whether it is a fantastic bottle of red wine he's home, a chocolate calendar or an invitation to a gourmet restaurant. I do not like the mandatory gifts and has such fine with dropping each other's Christmas gifts because earlier this year we had invested several thousand in a new piece of furniture for our home.

J. How can a man seduce you and make you feel comfortable in his company?

That he is himself that he is in no hurry to reach something, and not steely on the plan to succeed and the goal redeemed ... that there is room for both splitting with laughter, and foolish and still be serious.

***

Here is the answer to my questions as I asked for Camilla

A. What do you find sexy in a man?

It depends on the man. It can be many different things. Generally, it is of course never bad with the good looks but a balanced, masculine attitude and behavior can also do much by itself. He must not be feminine, but not stereotypical over-masculine. Intelligence I also find very appealing, and then I am as if so many other women unfortunately attracted complicated men. They should not be too easy, and it is allowed to be a "dark" in them, so you sense that there will be challenges associated with the relationship.

B. What part of a man do you gaze at first when you see

him for the first time!

The eyes and hands.

C. How can you be a sexy woman without him touching you!

We can easily. Flirt through conversation and with the eyes can be very sexy.

D. Which part of man you find most sexy?

His brain.

E. Can a contact be enough to awaken something in you (not an intimate place of your body)?

Yes. I would actually say that touch on non-intimate places may arouse more than touch on intimate places.

F. How do you like to be surprised?

With good food, like homemade, with good wine ... Common experiences such. Cinema or theater. Rather common experiences than gifts.

G. What fantasy would you rather see a man strip as?

I would rather not see a man strip.

H. What causes you to lose focus from a man what he

must do or say?

If he does not listen to me when I talk, and I sense it, he sits and waits for even being allowed to speak. If he goes close to my limits at the beginning of a relationship where he does not yet know them - it can, for example. Be at inappropriate humor at my expense etc..... These things can make me lose interest in a man in the initial phase.

I. **If a man shall deliver a gift or flowers, how to think it could be a little more interesting if it is possible to you?**

It is always great if it is a surprise. Otherwise, I will say that if you deliver a gift along with a few loving words or to clearly mark, the gift is associated with pleasure to the giver, then any gift better.

J. **How can a man seduce you and make you feel comfortable in his company?**

If he tells me something interesting about his thoughts and his life, which can enrich me, while listening to me when I tell. If he does not press too much, but at the same time clearly shows that he likes me. Moreover, if I sense he has a pride of his life and the things he does, and may provoke me a little and get me think in new ways. So, there is a good chance that I can find him seductively.

Here is the answer to my questions as I asked for Thomas

    A. What do you find sexy in a man?

Shirt less

    B. What part of a man do you gaze at first when you see him for the first time!

face

    C. How can you be a sexy woman without him touching you!

bulge in the pants

    D. Which part of man you find most sexy?

dick

    E. Can a contact be enough to awaken something in you (not an intimate place of your body)?

Yes

    F. How do you like to be surprised?

Kisses

    G. What fantasy would you rather see a man strip as?

I do not know

H. What causes you to lose focus from a man what he must do or say?

if he gets too technical, playing with dummies and other stupid word, it turns me completely

I. If a man shall deliver a gift or flowers, how to think it could be a little more interesting if it is possible to you?

I do not know

J. How can a man seduce you and make you feel comfortable in his company?

if he acts as if he really likes me. This is what I turn to.

***

Here is the answer to my questions as I asked for Jens

A. What do you find sexy in a man?

I think is sexy when you are that you have nice face and good ass and nice ass.

B. What part of a man do you gaze at first when you see him for the first time!

Gaze and eye contact and flirt.

C. How can you be a sexy woman without him touching you!

Smile in secret, talk to me and flirt with me.

D. Which part of man you find most sexy?

Good eye contact, respectable man.

E. Can a contact be enough to awaken something in you (not an intimate place of your body)?

Yes, it can, because I like the contact.

F. How do you like to be surprised?

I like to be surprised with good food and a little gift for me.

G. What fantasy would you rather see a man strip as?

Where I lie in bed, and she strips in front of me. And he will not touch me or I will not touch him. Very intimate.

H. What causes you to lose focus from a man what he must do or say?

When he behaves like an asshole

I. If a man shall deliver a gift or flowers, how to think it could be a little more interesting if it is possible to you?

Keep eye contact and giving good signal. If a man must hand over a gift or flowers, how to think it could be a little more interesting if it is possible to you: At dinnertime, or special day, as our brand today, and our first day. And he could give me the gift or flowers in front of my family or friends.

J. **How can a man seduce you and make you feel comfortable in his company?**

Keeps eye contact, and show that he is interested in me, he may be able to show that he likes me, even though we are surrounded by other people.

113

Acknowledgements!

I would really like to thank the following people for their work in my life and some of these people had an effect on the genesis of this book

Lennart Kiil.

I cannot but thank you deeply and mostly of the many lovely moments we used together. The many things we discussed. First and foremost is you actually inspired me to write this book. You gave me an opportunity to give your words to know when the manifesto existed. This option continued since you made Folkets Avis. (People's Newspaper) It is I who thank you for our unique friendship.

Allan Windekilde.

I have throughout my life met, many unique and lovely people, but you are definitely a gift that I in every way cannot thank enough for the many times you have given your time just to listen and see the world from different angles. I was pleased you took me as I was. I understand that your wife put so much value in you.

Bjarne Sinkjær.

I can only thank for the many hours we have had and yes, you have enriched me by your way of seeing the world and the human values that I so much appreciate. As no time is in short supply in this world and that you just as you are, the person you are.

Andreas J Søe.

I am often surprised and enriched over your way of being just as you are. It was surprising that you simply jumped into things and still remember when you just decided to start yoga together with me. Even then, I had not seen your surprise still with your loyalty and your good mood. Just as you are.

Liss Dirksen.

I know you as a person have not always had it easy, and when you tried to do the best for me even as a child. Although we see the world differently, and may disagree on many things, you will always be unique for me. Thank you for you are a good mother person.

Poul Bonde.

we have a truly unique friendship with so many good and unique experiences. I know that you are just there if I need it and you know I have not always been easy. Yes, I know I have a weakness for women starting their 20s and yes, I have since been allowed to hear again that I do it in a loving way.

Manni Bach.

I am grateful that you are part of my life and your way of seeing the world is an enrichment for me in so many ways. I would like to give a huge thank you for being who you are.

Greg and Charlotte Wolf.

I am so grateful for you two people in my life and I'm grateful that part of my dreams could become reality. Thank you for being in this part of my life. Thanks.

Thomas Ulrich.

93! your friendship is one of the must enriching that I have had in the short time we've known each other. You're like the brother I always wanted and again you brought so many good moments into our company. 93 93/93

This is an article from the largest rumor magazine, image to the left is the well-known blogger **Mascha Vang**, who elected me to the variety of images that were to choose from and on the right side the picture he appointed and as you can see, it is a picture of me!

118

THE BLACK SIGN

by Lars Rex Mundi

Another book by the author *Lars Rex Mundi*. **The Black Sign** is a conspiracy novel.

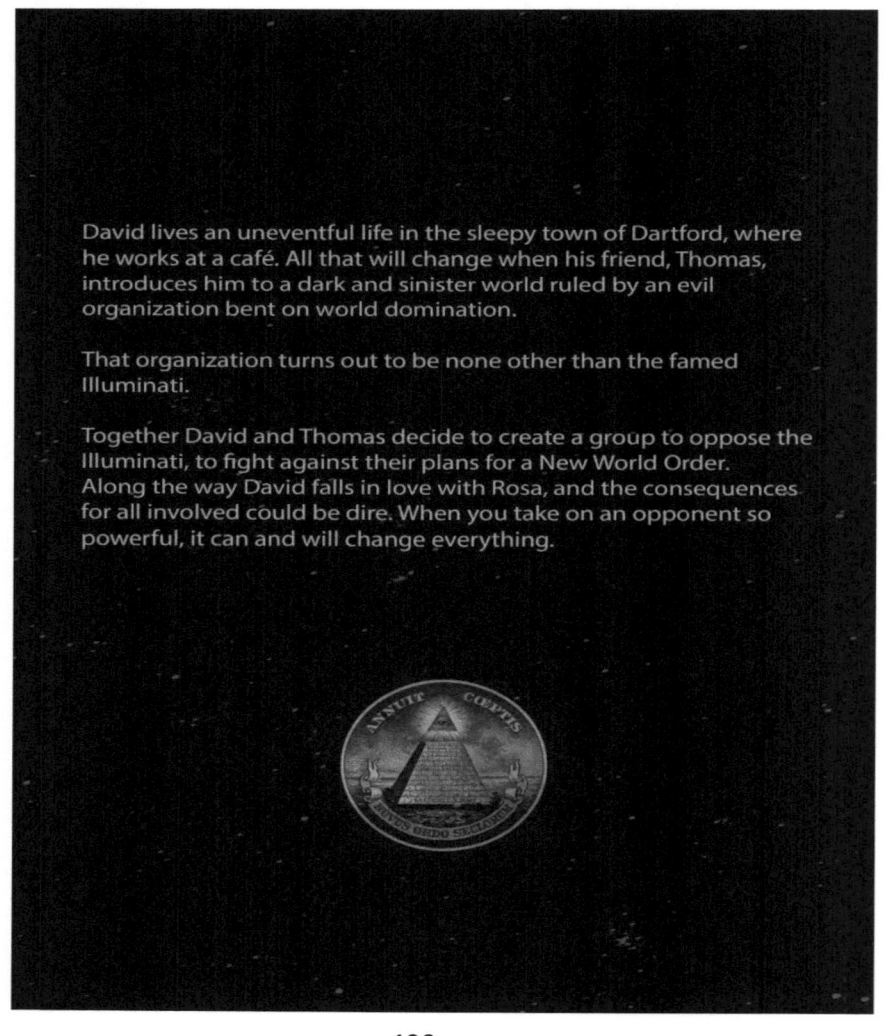

David lives an uneventful life in the sleepy town of Dartford, where he works at a café. All that will change when his friend, Thomas, introduces him to a dark and sinister world ruled by an evil organization bent on world domination.

That organization turns out to be none other than the famed Illuminati.

Together David and Thomas decide to create a group to oppose the Illuminati, to fight against their plans for a New World Order. Along the way David falls in love with Rosa, and the consequences for all involved could be dire. When you take on an opponent so powerful, it can and will change everything.